DIVORCE,
REMARRIAGE
& LEADERSHIP

LAW OR GOSPEL?

OKANAGAN
PUBLISHING CO.

ALAN J. NIEBERGAL

Published by:

www.OkanaganPublishingCo.ca

Okanagan Publishing Co (OKPC) is an imprint of

Okanagan Publishing Inc.
1024 Lone Pine Court
Kelowna, BC V1P 1M7
www.okanaganpublishinghouse.ca

All scripture quotations, unless otherwise indicated, are taken from the English Standard Version of the Bible, copyright@ 2001,2008,2016 by Crossway, a publishing ministry of Good News Publishers. | Scripture quotations marked NKJV are from the New King James Version of the Bible, copyright@ 1979,1980,1982 by Thomas Nelson Inc.

Printed in the United States of America

ISBN: 978-1-990389-19-1

Table of Contents

"Grace, strength, and peace to those going through a divorce and or remarriage and blessings in your marriage or singleness."

- Alan J. Niebergal

Introduction

How we deal with real-life issues has an impact on our life with the Lord and in our proclamation of the gospel. It also reveals a lot about ourselves and the state of our hearts and as well as determines whether we enter into God's fulness. The gospel is the good news of God in his love extending grace to us through the cross when He bore in Himself the penalty of our sin. The penalty of sin is death—spiritual death, physical death, and eternal death in hell. The result of sin is misery, darkness, guilt, slavery to sin, emptiness, hell, etc. This gift of God in the love of God in Jesus must be received to be actual in a person's life. It is not automatic. He bore the sin of those who receive him as Savior and Lord, who took on our sin on the cross and rose from the dead to give us eternal and abundant life. The benefits of being born again are forgiveness, peace, joy, love, fulness, strength, heaven, etc.

His grace in Jesus is far beyond what man might think or imagine. Likewise, if we don't extend grace, after receiving grace in Christ Jesus, we may have received grace in vain. We may have not actually received grace, grasped grace, appreciated, applied it, and or understand it. As the Apostle Paul says, "But by the grace of God I am what I am, and his grace toward me was not in vain. On the contrary, I worked harder than any of them, though it was not I, but the grace of God that is with me" (1 Corinthians 15:10). We also must let Christ's fullness direct and empower our lives. It is important that our actions match our right doctrine. To have a doctrine that is inconsistent with the message does great harm to everyone. This applies to all of us.

The issue of divorce and remarriage is very controversial in the church, that is why many churches refuse to deal with it. There are many views on this doctrinal and ethical issue. (1) One view believes that if you divorce you should never remarry. (2) The second view believes that if you divorce you can only remarry if you are the innocent party and your spouse has committed adultery and only the innocent party can remarry. (3) The third view believes that there are two reasons or cases that could lead to divorce. As the Westminster Confession of faith states adultery and desertion are the only legitimate reason for divorce and remarriage. (4) The fourth approach states that there are other cases where divorce and thus remarriage are legitimate. (5) The fifth case believes in no-fault divorce and that divorce and remarriage are totally legitimate in all cases. How we apply the grace and truth revealed in God's Word in regards to this issue is critical to applying what the Bible teaches and is Jesus' way of grace, wisdom, life, justice, truth, holiness, and love.

Because this issue is so controversial many churches have hidden agendas about this issue. They just don't talk about it, although, their approach is felt and observed in how they treat or neglect those who are divorced and remarried. To be fair, I am referring primarily to Evangelical churches. Evangelical means to preach, teach and live, the good news of the gospel.

Divorce, remarriage, and leadership are complicated issues. Those who don't approach it theologically taking into consideration what Jesus had to say in relation to the whole Bible often jump to conclusions that are convenient for them. As with this issue, much Theology or sound doctrine is neglected first because it is difficult and secondly because it can cause division if not approached with the grace that should be attached to it, or even if it is approached with grace. For many, it is too hard a work to fully engage in and too messy to care about restoring those found in the situation of divorce and remarriage and thus dealing with the different views of the people in the church. The church often just wants to play it safe and keep control and avoid controversy. They don't want to take the risk. They would rather hide their talents. (Matthew 25:14-30) Many churches are too safe to actually love. Fortunately, there are some who know how to hold grace and truth together, especially as it relates to this issue. Jesus said, "For whoever would save his life will lose it, but whoever loses his life for my sake will find it" (Matthew 16:25). The church in general is playing it too safe and losing its life.

How does God deal with those who do not measure up to the ideal? (Isaiah 46:3) That ideal is Jesus who was fully holy and without sin. Does Jesus toss them to the side and choose to forsake them? He may set them aside for a time, but our God is one who is primarily interested in restoration. He most profoundly restores people in Salvation as an example for us to follow in sharing the gospel and living it out. If a person is truly one of His elect, he never forsakes them. (2 Peter 1:10) However, if that person will not learn what God wants them to learn he may set them aside from leadership until they do. Let it not be the immature church that sets them aside, but God that sets them aside.

How has God dealt with people who have failed? How did he deal with Peter when Peter denied Jesus in his hour of need? How did he deal with Moses, Abraham, Jonah, David, Solomon, etc.? Surely, none of these had a past that who *above reproach*. God not only extends grace in salvation but every day in our lives. It is also honoring God when God's people do likewise and dishonoring God when they do not. After all, it is primarily all about God and thus Jesus.

Providentially God may have blessed you with a healthy Christian family heritage, a good temperament, and good friends and opportunities. Not everyone comes from the same place. Some have many great challenges and in spite of these challenges forge ahead and learn and build upon their mistakes and failures. Could we not have a little compassion without self-righteousness? What do we have that didn't come from God? Could we not be thankful without condescending to others?

Jesus said, "Blessed are the merciful, for they shall receive mercy" (Matthew 5:7). It is likely that you might fail in the future, would not you want people to be merciful to you when that occurs? Many of those who accomplish great things usually have failed many times before bearing an abundance of fruit. (John 15: -1-17) If we extend mercy to people, it is more likely they will extend grace to us. "Though he falls, he shall not be cast headlong, for the Lord upholds his hand" (Psalm 37:24). If God does this, are we not to follow His lead?

CHAPTER ONE
The Context

To interpret the Bible correctly we must interpret it in context. We must consider the whole to understand the part. The Bible must be understood as a whole to fathom the complexities of truth and let them be put together in our minds and hearts and our teaching. As stated previously people avoid studying the Bible because it is difficult and complex at times. However, understanding the context in which the scripture is written is the first rule of Biblical interpretation which theologians call hermeneutics. Hermeneutics is the principles of interpretation. We must also consider the culture and time period it is written in and the historical context as well as what kind of literature is it. Is it historical, poetic, allegorical, hyperbole, an analogy, metaphorical, apocalyptic, didactic indicative, literal and etc.? "The orthodox Protestant hermeneutic follows Martin Luther's view of *sensus literalis*. There is much confusion today regarding the "literal sense" of Scripture. Luther means that one should interpret the Bible according to the manner in which it was written, or in its "literary sense. "This was an attempt to prevent fanciful flights into subjectivism by which the Scriptures are turned into a "wax nose," twisted and shaped according to the interpreter's whim or bias. To guard against subjectivism, Luther sought a rule that would guide the interpreter to an objective rendering of the text. To interpret the Bible "literally" in the classical sense requires that we learn to recognize in Scripture different genres of literature."[1]

This is not a book on hermeneutics which is a very important aspect and essential study to be a good steward of the Bible. Perhaps a book like Bernard Ramm's book, *Protestant Biblical Interpretation*, would be helpful.

To understand what Jesus said on Divorce and remarriage we first must set it in the context which is the whole Biblical revelation which includes the Old Testament. Too often today, Christians read and study only the New Testament. Without the context of the Old Testament, we are freewheeling—cut loose from the mooring—drifting to whatever place the current of

1 R.C. Sproul, *The Last Days According to Jesus,* (Grand Rapids: Baker Books,1998) 65

convenience takes us. We need God's full revelation as the context to interpret the Bible. The Bible itself assists us in interpreting the Bible. Scripture helps us understand scripture. We fully understand the New Testament in understanding the Old Testament and discerning the continuity and discontinuity—of the law and the gospel.

The understanding of the law and gospel is severely lacking in today's evangelical church. The law tells us how we fall short and the extent of what sin is. Jesus expands our understanding of sin and the extent of God's blessings in the beatitudes and his teaching. The law tells us about our need and the gospel tells us of remedy in God by He Himself taking the penalty of our sin on the cross as the good news, by which people can be redeemed. Unless we understand the bad news, we will not fully appreciate or enter into the good news. William Perkins in his book, *The Art of Prophesying*, makes this really clear. Where are the preaching and teaching today that includes the law and the gospel? It seems the legalist emphasizes the law with an overemphasis and the antinominalist or liberal emphasizes too much the grace of the gospel or the good news without the context of the law.

We must also understand the culture that Jesus spoke to and the issues of his day he was addressing before we can make the application to our day. What did it say to people in his culture is critical to understanding and interpreting what he was saying and its implications for interpretation and in making the application to our lives today?

CHAPTER TWO
Remarriage in the Old Testament

In the Old Testament, divorce and remarriage were allowed and it was legal. Would God give instruction to his people to do what is illegal or not according to God's law in the Old Testament—as interpreted by some on the issue of divorce and remarriage when he legitimized divorce and remarriage? This is what it says in Deuteronomy in the Old Testament:

> *"When a man takes a wife and marries her if then she finds no favor in his eyes because he has found some* indecency in her, *and he writes her a certificate of divorce and puts it in her hand and sends her out of his house, and she departs out of his house, and if she goes and becomes another man's wife, and the latter man hates her and writes her a certificate of divorce and puts it in her hand and sends her out of his house, or if the latter man dies, who took her to be his wife, then*

her former husband, who sent her away, may not take her again to be his wife after she has been defiled, for that is an abomination before the Lord. And you shall not bring sin upon the land that the Lord your God is giving you for an inheritance." (Deuteronomy 24:1-4)

I would like to especially point out two things. First is that it is quite open-ended—there is a lot of room for interpretation when God's word says, "she finds no favor in his eyes because he has found some indecency in her." This is the issue that the people of Jesus' day were disputing and we will consider it in a little more in detail later. Why would he find no favor in her? Was it because she didn't cook very well or clean, or always nagged? Was it because she was flirting with other men? Was it because she was very manipulative and perhaps controlling? Was she not loyal? Was she quarrelsome or fretful? (Proverbs 21:19) It seems like there is a lot of room for discretion for the man in applying this instruction. Certainly, there could also be a lot of room for abuse in how this was applied.

Secondly, what is the indecency to be found in her? The Old Testament emphasizes what God lays out which is against God's law, His holiness which includes sins of commission or omission. The New Testament emphasizes God's extension of grace. The punishment for sin in the Old Testament was in relation to what was the extent and severity of the sin. We would not fully know the gospel if we don't know how we have broken God's law. If we don't understand the law, we will never fully understand or appreciate the gospel. There are many sins that are indecent, some much more than others. Homosexuality (the act not necessarily the tendency) or bestiality, adultery, fornication, sodomy, etc., etc., would be indecent according to the Bible. Some are more indecent than others, according to their punishment of them in the Old Testament. What other indecencies could there be? Could it involve a wife disrespecting her husband in public and in private—perhaps sharing some very private matters with inappropriate persons, defrauding, being disloyal, etc.? Again, there is a lot of room for liberty and abuse in the application of the term indecency in ordinary and everyday life.

For the woman in that culture, the options were limited. If divorced they could go back to live with their parents, find someone else to marry, or go into some other form of work or prostitution.

Of course, since the time of Jesus things have become more equitable between men and women. Women now have equal status and dignity in marriage, although since the beginning this has always been God's intention. Even though men and women are equal they may have different roles in marriage and in church leadership according to the Bible. (Genesis 3:16; 1 Timothy 2:12) This means in a brief statement that a woman should not be the Senior pastor of a church or the main denominational leader or a professor of Theology in a seminary. The man is primarily responsible to be the spiritual leader and is called to set an example in Christlikeness. (Ephesians 5:25) As the husband is submissive to Christ's Lordship, he should be an example to his wife, so that she would also walk in Christ's love and Lordship.[1] The Bible instructs the wife to be submissive to the husband but also instructs the wife and husband to be submissive to each other in love. (Ephesians 5:21-22) To be submissive is to respect that person and the responsibility they bear in leadership or in life or with respect due to all people who are all created in God's image. The husband should especially set an example of being submissive to the Lord and honoring the Lord. This is how he is to primarily lead. Together

---

1 John Pipe &Wayne Grudem, ed., *Recovering Biblical Manhood and Womanhood*, (Wheaton IL.: Crossway, 2012)

they learn to trust and submit to His perfect and loving will and grow in their love for Him and one another. The family should also follow Christ's loving Lordship.

There is an overemphasis on equality today. Satan tempted Adam and Eve with being equal to God. However, there is no comparison. We are far from being God. "Therefore, we do not do Theology as gods or as equals of God, but as his creation."[2] An employee and a CEO of a company are equal in dignity but they have different roles and different weights of responsibility. We have emphasized too much equality and not enough responsibility. (Genesis 3:16)

Women can divorce and remarry at will and often receive at least half of the assets. Hopefully, the divorce is fair to both parties. This would be the Christ-like way of doing things. Christians should not need to go to court but should be fair in how divorce is conducted. (1 Corinthians 6:1-8) However, if people harden their hearts the courts may be necessary.

The point is that in the Old Testament people legally divorced and remarried as they also did in Jesus'

---

2 Joe R. Beeke and Paul M. Smalley, *Reformed Systematic Theology*, vol. 1, (Wheaton, Illinois: Crossway, 2019) 69

cultural and historical time period. The disciples asked Jesus, "Why then did Moses command one to give a certificate of divorce and to send her away? He said to them, "Because of your hardness of heart Moses allowed you to divorce your wives, but from the beginning, it was no so" (Matthew 19:7-8). What does it mean to have a hard heart? Can God's people harden their hearts today?

To harden our hearts is to know God's will and refuse to do it. Refusing to do God's will over time will harden your heart like callouses on our hands from hard work. Like clay in the sun. It becomes hard and brittle and breaks. (Proverbs 6:15) The Bible wisely says, "He who is often reproved, yet stiffens his neck, will suddenly be broken and that without healing" (Proverbs 29:1). We can also harden our hearts through bitterness. God's word says, "See to it that no one fails to obtain the grace of God; that no "root of bitterness" springs up and causes trouble, and by it many become defiled" (Hebrews 12:15). Bitterness can affect even a Christian and it corrupts much of our inner and outer life in Christ and greatly harms themselves and other people. If someone becomes bitter in a marriage or in life it will cause great harm. Ultimately, we are each responsible for whether we become bitter or better.

There are many examples of hardening of the heart in the scripture but the best warnings of it are in the book of Hebrews in the Bible. God had told the people of God Israel to enter the promised land and that he would go with them so that they would be victorious in the fight to conquer the land. The people thought the odds were against them and refused to enter the promised land as God had instructed. They harden the heart against the Lord and God brought judgment. That generation went back into the wilderness for 40 years and died off and the next generation went into the promised land. It was like they were saying to God, "We don't like that plan, can you propose another one? God, we would like to dictate to you. When it suits us, we will let you know."

"Therefore, as the Holy Spirit says,

> *'Today, if you hear his voice,*
> *do not harden your hearts as in the rebellion,*
> *on the day of testing in the wilderness,*
> *where your fathers put me to the test*
> *and saw my works for forty years.*
> *Therefore I was provoked with that generation,*
> *and said, 'They always go astray in their heart;*
> *they have not known my ways.'*

As I swore in my wrath,
'They shall not enter my rest.'"

Take care, brothers, lest there be in any of you an evil, unbelieving heart, leading you to fall away from the living God. But exhort one another every day, as long as it is called "today," that none of you may be hardened by the deceitfulness of sin." (Hebrews 3:7-13)

In the Old Testament, divorce and remarriage were allowed, it was legal. "God was providing a partial remedy for the harm that a hard-hearted husband or wife could do to the other person in the marriage." [3]

In a marriage, you do not know if your spouse will harden their heart through bitterness, stubbornness, pride, or other deceitful practices of sin. People are still hardening their hearts today. Truly a Christian should be free from this hardening, but God does not take away our free will and people can fall into sin, especially by the sophisticated justification of the deceitfulness of sin and thus their approach to life. One needs to examine our life to see if we are truly in Christ if bitterness is a large part

---

3 Wayne Grudem, *What the Bible Says About Divorce and Remarriage*, (Wheaton Illinois: Crossway, 2021) 20

of our life. "Therefore, brothers, be all the more diligent to confirm your calling and election" (2 Peter 1:10).

Bitterness can be resolved by walking in the Spirit, becoming more Christlike, and forgiveness of those who have harmed you and forgiving yourself. Conflict resolution often is not exemplified in families but it is a skill that can be learned to avoid falling into bitterness. We need to seek to resolve conflict if possible.[4] As the Bible says, "If possible, so far as it depends on you, live peaceably with all" (Romans 12:18). Conflict resolution is an art that can be learned.

In this Old Testament revelation by God, he instructs that if someone divorces his wife and he goes she remarries someone else if her husband dies or that husband, she was now married to her divorces her, the first husband cannot take back the wife he divorced and remarry her. The point that he is making is that we are not to take divorce lightly and that we are not to abuse it as a means of manipulation, selfishness, or pride. This instruction was to try to limit somewhat the abuse of

---

4 Douglas Stone, Bruce Patton, Sheila Heen, *Difficult Conversations: How to Discuss What Matters Most,* (New York, New York: Penquin Group, 2000)

divorce and remarriage and to establish restrictions on its abuse as a form of manipulation or pride.

Of course, even in those times, people would observe the damaging effects of divorce. People would count the cost of their actions because it would harm a family although ideally the family relationships would be restored and forgiveness and mercy would again be mutual in the family.

CHAPTER THREE
The Ideals of Marriage

Jesus in New Testament states the ideals of marriage and talks about the issue of divorce in these scriptures in synoptic gospels. (Matthew 5:31-32; 19:1-12; Mark 10:11-12; Luke 16:18) In Mark and Luke there is just one statement about divorce stating that if you divorce and remarry you commit adultery. In Matthew, the context is elaborated. The "Pharisees came up to him (Jesus) and tested him by asking, "Is it lawful to divorce one's wife for any cause?" (Matthew 19:3). They were asking him to weigh into the debate about the just reasons to divorce. They wanted him to side in with the two different schools of thought at his time.

Jesus doesn't fall into their trap of getting things lost in controversy where they are looking for excuses, and missing the main point. He states the ideal very strongly. Basically, He is saying we should not be looking for excuses to divorce but remain in a marriage if at all possible and only in the very extreme cases where a spouse is committing some immoral sexual sin continually divorce was allowed and remarriage was allowed, as it was in Old Testament. The focus is on the ideal of staying in a covenant relationship because this is God's ideal. If we really consider the extent of the covenant Jesus in essence is saying then it would be like metaphorically committing adultery to remarry. However, this stated hyperbole it is similar to equating lust with committing adultery. (Matthew 5:27-28) Everyone has lusted at least once.

By his statement in Matthew 19:1-9, Jesus does away with polygamy and stresses that we are to take marriage very seriously and sacredly. One wonders why God would not restrict polygamy in the Old Testament. This is a question of God's Providence and God working in human history according to His divine wisdom, foreknowledge, His all-knowing purposes, goodness, and power, and man's ability to learn God's ways. However, Jesus deals with this issue now and states God's intended ideal in marriage as monogamous since creation:

"Because of your hardness of heart Moses allowed you to divorce your wives, but from the beginning, it was not

so. And I say to you: whoever divorces his wife, except for sexual immorality and marries another commits adultery. The disciples said to him, "If such is the case with his wife, it is better not to marry." But he said to them, "Not everyone can receive this saying, but only those to whom it is given. For there are eunuchs who have been so from birth, and there are eunuchs who have been made eunuchs by men, and there are eunuchs who have made themselves eunuchs for the sake of the kingdom of heaven. Let the one who is able to receive this receive it" (Matthew 19:8-12).

He is saying that we should not just divorce and remarry out of pride and selfishness. Also, according to the ideal of marriage, this is breaking a covenant bond. According to the ideal, it is like committing adultery just like lusting after a woman or a woman lusting after a man. (Matthew 5:27-28)

Some people, understand that only the innocent party can divorce and remarry. The guilty party the one who committed adultery is not free to remarry and if they do, they are committing adultery. In the Old Testament, the punishment for adultery was death. Let's set this in context. The word used for the translated phrase, "except on the ground of sexual immorality" (Matthew 5:32; Matthew 19:9), in Greek the original language of the

New Testament, the Greek word porneia is translated as sexual immorality. Porneia in the Greek means all unlawful sexual sin, including incest, bestiality, homosexuality, lesbianism, pedophilia, etc. So, in this context, it would not be only adultery that could necessarily lead to divorce. In the Old Testament people divorced for many reasons and remarried and it was totally legal. God is the same God in the Old Testament as in the New Testament. His morals and his holiness and or goodness does not change. Therefore, to remarry is thus to commit adultery cannot be the right understanding of what Jesus said, for Jesus spoke in the context of the previous revelation in the Bible. Is Jesus using hyperbole when he says a person commits adultery when they marry again? Only if we understand the context will we understand what he is saying and get the main point that Jesus is talking about. If Jesus allowed for divorce and remarriage in certain cases would there not also be other cases where it would be allowed? We will explore this a little later.

Also in Jesus' time, the punishment for adultery was death by stoning according to the Old Testament. However, Jesus reinforces this expansion of grace with the women caught in adultery. (John 8:1-1) If Jesus expands his grace why is there a tendency among his people to shrink it? Do we want grace for ourselves and justice for other people? Oftentimes, what it comes down to is, that those who are unaffected do not care.

What does he mean then that the person who marries commits adultery? What Jesus is saying here in context is "Jesus is saying that a man who wrongly divorces his wife and has not received a legitimate divorce and is in fact still married to his original wife at the time he initiates the second marriage."[1] In God's ideal, this would be the case if the person was not legitimately divorced. A legitimate divorce is a legal divorce. This is how serious one should take the issue of divorce. It should be for legitimate grounds and we will consider the legitimate grounds of divorce and remarriage a little later. "Nowhere does the Bible say that divorce itself is adultery."[2] The disciples "jumped to the conclusion that it would be safer never to get married than to be stuck in an unhappy marriage for one's whole life."[3]

In the times of Jesus, there were two schools of thought in the Jewish Pharisaical group of Jewish

---

1 Ibid, 21

2 Ibid, 55

3 Ibid, 21

scholars. The debate especially had to do with the words in Deuteronomy about the interpretation of the phrase, "something indecent in her." The conservative school called the Shammai interpreted it to mean adultery or any sexual immorality. Yet according to the Old Testament, the consequence of adultery was death by stoning as were some other indecent sins. Because Israel at the time of Jesus was under Roman rule, they were not allowed to practice this aspect of God's law in the Old Testament, nor did the Jews previous to this when they were not under Roman rule practice this, by in large. The more Liberal group called the Hillel group believed the indecency even involved failing to cook the husband's meal properly." The School of Hillel, however, says that a man may divorce his wife even if she has merely ruined his food as it is written, "because he finds something indecent about her." (Gittin 9:10)

It seemed like Jesus was siding with the Shammai Pharisaical school. Similarly, many have sided with that Shammai school today. However, Jesus was making the point that you have to have a very good reason to divorce and it should not be taken lightly. There should be legitimate reasons for divorce and all other avenues should have been taken to avoid it. Jesus states the ideal of marriage. Would He do less? This is especially true because the gospel of Matthew is set in the context of the beatitudes. (Matthew 5:32) Here Jesus states the important ideal. "You have heard that it was said to those of old, "You shall not murder, and whoever murders will be liable to judgment. But I say to you that everyone who is angry with his brother will be liable to judgment; whoever insults his brother will be liable to the council; and whoever says, "You fool!' will be liable to the hell of fire (Matthew 5:21-22) Those who are angry with someone have committed murder in their heart, which might in time lead to the action. Should a person be convicted of murder because they were angry in this way? Jesus stresses the importance of keeping your heart and that all evil things stem from the heart. "For out of the heart come evil thoughts, murder, adultery, sexual immorality, theft, false witness, slander" (Matthew 15:19). We can interpret scripture legalistically or we set it in the context of grace and interpret it with the heart of Jesus who speaks to the deeper issues and matters of the heart. Sometimes life is very complex and does not fit in easy answers and approaches. Because God is holy the ideal is his standard, but all people fall short of His holiness. This should not be used as an excuse, but just understood to be a fact. God as we walk with Him is in the process of purifying our hearts—our desires, making us a vessel to display his holiness and thus his glory. (2 Timothy 2:21)

Martin Luther was often very proficient as well as succinct in looking at the whole and getting to the heart of the issue. He said, "*When Jesus spoke on divorce, he was not legislating the issue, but preaching against a capricious use of divorce laws.*" To be capricious is to be given to unaccountable changes of mood or behavior. It means to divorce on a whim, anger, bitterness, or a sinful pride issue. Many interpret what Jesus said as legislating the issue of divorce and remarriage. They then tend to approach the whole issue of marriage, divorce, and leadership from the issue that Jesus instituted a new law. This in my opinion is the approach of the legalist. Legalism is the way of the Pharisees and it is not attractive. Legalism even disguised really stinks. Could it be possible that the Old Testament law encouraged more grace than Jesus? Jesus certainly extends grace and expands it to the woman caught in the act of adultery and in speaking to the woman at the well that had five husbands and was not married to the man she was now living with. (John 4:17) He exposed her sin but did not exclude her from grace. That is what the law does—it exposes sin, so the remedy in Christ may be appropriated. "For by the works of the law no human being will be justified in his sight, since through the law comes the knowledge of sin" (Romans 3:20).

CHAPTER FOUR

God Hates Divorce

God says in his word: *"For the LORD God of Israel says That He hates divorce, for it covers one's garment with violence," Says the LORD of hosts. "Therefore, take heed to your spirit, that you do not deal treacherously"* (Malachi 2:16; NKJV).

God hates the brokenness and misery of sin that divorce brings. He hates the harm done to all involved. It breaks a love covenant that two people had and, in a sense, the union has failed. Each will have to live with the failure and hopefully learn from it and build upon it and move forward. It causes pain to the couple, to the children, to the extended family, and friends, and somewhat to society. However, even with these failures, God can turn the experience toward good. As the Bible says, "And we know that for those who love God all things work together for good, for those who are called according to his purpose" (Romans 8:28).

God hates the hardness of heart, that bitterness, envy, and pride that results in divorce and the harm it causes to the people involved and others. Sin works against everything that may be good in our lives. Let us be clear—sin ultimately brings misery. We also need to be forgiven in Christ (1 John 1:9) and to forgive ourselves and forge ahead in Christian growth, service, and spiritual formation. "Failure isn't so bad if it doesn't attack the heart. Success is all right if it doesn't go the head." Grantland Rice. "One reason that God created time was that there would be a place to bury the failures of the past." James Long.[1]

Israel hardened their hearts against God and played fast and loose with idols and thought God should be okay with it. After all, he is big enough to handle it. God brought judgment on the nation, by the conquering of Israel by a wicked nation. They were taken into captivity in Babylon a foreign land for 70 years. After that judgment on Israel, the nation learned to take a lot more seriously God and his law and this was then the context of the coming of Christ. The religious teachers of that time were especially concerned about keeping God's law

1 John H. Maxwell, *Failing Forward*, (Nashville Tennessee: Thomas Nelson, 2000) 23,73.

and avoiding God's judgment and hopefully ushering in the coming of God's kingdom.

God will judge a nation that does not honor him and he will discipline those who are truly his people. God says in his word, "For the moment all discipline seems painful rather than pleasant, but later it yields the peaceful fruit of righteousness to those who have been trained by it" (Hebrews 12:5) "But when we are judged by the Lord, we are disciplined so that we may not be condemned along with the world" (1 Corinthians 11:32). "For it is time for judgment to begin at the household of God; and if it begins with us, what will be the outcome for those who do not obey the gospel of God?" (1 Peter 4:17).

God is concerned about what we do, but he is mostly interested in who we are. He desires to refine in the fire of his holy love and remove those sinful tendencies that bring misery, destruction, and harm. Those deep heart issues like selfishness, pride, envy, lust, etc. God's ultimate purpose for us is to experience and live in the full union with God and to have a pure heart so that we might receive the fullness of God. "And to know the love of Christ that surpasses knowledge, that you may be filled with the fulness of God" (Ephesians 3:19). Yes, God wants you to have knowledge of Him and His word, but he also wants you to experience him in his fulness deep within our heart's desires. Jesus said, "Blessed are the pure in heart for they shall see God" (Matthew 5:8). Purity of heart is a process of spiritual formation that a Christian is in, all their lives.

God hates divorce because of the harm it brings. Those who have been through a divorce know firsthand the pain it brings and they need those who will walk with them, support them as people, and not be intrusive because it is so complex and so sensitive an issue. When something like a divorce happens two things may be going on with other people in the church, with friends, acquaintances, and the world around them. One is because human nature is curious, people will ask questions about why it happened, even though they may not have a close relationship with the person. People are curious about what happened and they think they are ministering to the person if they ask them about the details. This may satisfy their curiosity, but it may just heap harm on the one going through the crisis. The other factor is compassion and people think they are being compassionate by being curious. They way too often are not. We do not naturally know how to minister to people emotionally and supportively, but we can learn. This is where some basic counseling or compassion or empathy skills are helpful.

We also need to be sensitive to the leading of the Holy Spirit in ministry. No one likes to explain to people how things have failed in a marriage and how they may have failed. Why do people think they are priests and those in this situation want people to confess to them and be accountable to them? Let them go first. Let them first confess their failings and shortcomings.

If people want to talk about the details, they will bring it up. Most people do not have many compassion skills or counseling or empathy skills, to be trusted with a heart. It is no fun for people to play counselor when they have no skills and are just intrusive because they are curious. Besides, it may take hours to explain the complexity of each situation, and often people don't make the time or truly listen. No one likes to be judged with only a brief understanding of the situation or integrated as if they are in a court of law. How many times and to how many people do you have to tell your story that only want a brief synopsis in two sentences and then they are okay with then making their judgment? It is helpful to just walk with people and be their friends and listen when they want to share.

CHAPTER FIVE

God Divorces Israel

Although divorce is not good, it may at times be necessary and God recognizes this. People may harden their hearts and continue in sin, even though there has been patience in the situation. People have a free choice. God doesn't force people against their will. God divorced Israel even though, God was extremely patient with Israel.

As it says in his word: *"She saw that for all the adulteries of that faithless one, Israel, I had sent her away with a decree of divorce. Yet her treacherous sister Judah did not fear, but she too went and played the whore"* (Jeremiah 3:8). At this time Israel was split into two kingdoms. The northern kingdom was called Israel and the southern kingdom was called Judah. The Northern Kingdom consisted of all the other ten tribes. The tribes of Benjamin and Judah made up the Southern kingdom.

God says here that he is going to divorce the Northern Kingdom. They continued to play fast and loose with God and worshipped idols, forsook God and his law, and were greatly immoral. God had given them hundreds of years, but they refused to repent and turn to God.

The tribe of Judah is the lineage of Jesus. Today we still call this southern tribe Israel and so does the Bible as well as in the New Testament. Some people think that the church has completely replaced Israel, but the Bible portrays in Romans Chapters 9-11 that Israel has not been replaced but expanded with the inclusion of Gentiles. The Kingdom of Israel, however, now is primarily spiritual. Israel and the Gentiles have been joined into one stream. A stream that includes all those who are of the elect in Christ. "And in this way, all Israel will be saved" (Romans 11:26). All the elect will come to saving faith. If we are not in Christ whether Jew or Gentile we are not of the elect. (John 3:3-5) As God's word again says, "For not all who are descended from Israel belong to Israel" (Romans 9:6). Israel is now primarily the spiritual elect in Christ.

God expanded his covenant to include the Gentiles as Romans chapter 9-11 emphasizes. Of course, this was God's plan all along. This is the mystery hidden from our sight for ages. "This mystery is that the Gentiles are fellow heirs, members of the same body, and partakers of the promise in Christ Jesus through the gospel" (Ephesians 3:6).

God in another place instructs God's people to divorce their non-Jewish wives. This also is a good reason why Christians are not to marry non-Christians. "She is free to marry to whom she wishes, only in the Lord" (1 Corinthians 7:39) If they are already married they are to seek to remain married. (1 Corinthians 7:10) In the time of Ezra God gave the command to divorce their foreign wives. Here is what God says:

"And Ezra the priest stood up and said to them, "You have broken faith and married foreign women, and so increased the guilt of Israel. Now then make confession to the Lord, the God of your fathers, and do his will. Separate yourselves from the peoples of the land and from the foreign wives" (Ezra 10:10-11).

This would have been very difficult to do. To preserve the nation and mankind at this time in history God required something very difficult. Moses in God's word had instructed them previously not to marry non-Jewish people.

Was God asking them to commit adultery because it would mean that they would remarry? This book should answer that question. If the divorce was legal, they could remarry. Why did God want the people to divorce their foreign wives which would occur if they separated from them? Why didn't God address this with Solomon when he married so many foreign wives? We are not on the committee for how and when God does things according to the mystery of His Providence and His progressive revelation that man might come to maturity and be ready for the revelation in Jesus Christ. Let us consider some factors theologically; God chose a nation called Israel to reveal himself and his grace to Israel and all people. He preserved his people in his providence so that mankind would not again like in the days of Noah be saturated in evil and wickedness. (Genesis 6:5) In the time of Ezra God had brought his people back from captivity in Babylon because God in his judgment allowed a wicked nation to judge God's people. This captivity lasted 70 years. It seemed that after this judgment the Jewish people had learned not to worship idols and to largely follow God's law. This is why during the time of Jesus that the Pharisees and others were concerned about keeping God's law and not worshipping idols. God most likely instructed the people of God at this time to divorce their foreign wives because foreign wives usually meant worshiping gods of other nations which were only idols. God was preserving his people from their own self-destruction. (Deuteronomy 7:3-4) Sin does bring self-destruction and darkness.

CHAPTER SIX
Practical Applications

As mentioned, there are many views on the issue of divorce and remarriage. I have chosen the fourth view for biblical and theological reasons. I believe theologically the Bible teaches that there are various *cases* in which divorce and that remarriage could occur and it is legal according to God's law. It is not a sin to remarry according to God's word, the Bible.

Nothing so practical has been so controversial in the church as the issue of divorce and remarriage, especially among evangelicals. If we don't look at this issue theologically in relation to the full revelation of God in the Bible and hasten to judgment, we may heap harm upon harm and affect our true Christian witness of the grace of God even while upholding the ideal. Perhaps this is why divorced and remarried people have remained in the background as second-class citizens in the church, not permitted in actual practice to preach and teach in the church. Perhaps this is why some divorced people are not totally comfortable in some churches. They sense the attitudes as they get to know church people. They can become members and participate, but often in some churches not all, they cannot be teachers, pastors, or preach. Even if they don't want to teach or preach, they are treated as second-class citizens, although it might not be the church's official policy. It, however, is the church's attitude on this issue, which is eventually picked up.

There are basically two approaches to dealing with Christians who may have fallen short of the standards upheld by God. The first approach is to not believe in full restoration only partial restoration. Divorced and remarried people are free to attend church or Bible study, be members, and such, but they are not to be a place of leadership, preach and or teach. Often churches don't say this, but this is their practice. They are not in the business of full restoration they are in the business of upholding a misunderstood man-made standard, somewhat similar to the Pharisees.

What kind of example are we setting they might say and think if we allow someone who has been divorced and remarried to be in leadership and or preach and teach? The world would think we are hypocrites. *What is better to be thought a hypocrite by the world or by God?* We can be focused on appearance like the world or we can be focused on the substance of Christ and his ways in restoration. Life is messy and we are not to just smooth over things and discard people because it destroys the image we want to present. Our image should be in Christ. Jesus said, "Do not judge by appearance but judge with right judgment" (John 7:24). If we don't practice the grace given to us in Christ, how are we to model it to each other and the world? We have truly then, received God's grace in vain, at least to a certain extent.

Some might say or think, how can I listen to someone preach who has been divorced and remarried? I can't see past their failure. They might also have a problem listening to the Apostle Peter who denied his Lord in his hour of Jesus' greatest need. King David who wrote most of the beautiful Psalms committed murder and adultery. I guess King David should not apply to be the pastor of most evangelical churches. Yet God fully restored David, through a process he took him through. Moses killed an Egyptian and buried him in the sand to try to avoid being exposed and had to run for his life. We can go on and on. God is very interested in restoration and displaying his glory in that process. It is sad when God's people are not interested also in it, since God in Christ restores us to full fellowship with the Father. We have followed the world, especially today in its cancel and woke culture. We have sought to appease the world rather than please Jesus. Of course, much discernment and wisdom are required in this process of restoring people.

Often church people are okay if a hard-core biker converts to Christianity and is soundly converted by the hand of God if they teach and preach and rightly so, but the church is very hesitant to extend grace to those who stumble as Christians. It would be helpful if the church had as one of the core committees a *restoration committee* and this committee learned to practice Biblical restoration. Their objective would be to work alongside God in restoration. Yes, there must often be time involved in the process and accountability but the committee's approach is primarily not punitive but restorative. Then we would truly be stewards of each other in Christ. "Brothers, if anyone is caught in any transgression, you who are spiritual should restore him in a spirit of gentleness. Keep watch on yourself, lest you too be tempted" (Galatians 6:1) We can easily be tempted with pride and self-righteousness. This temptation does also occur by not getting involved or criticizing from the sidelines. This certainly does also occur to those not fully dedicated to Jesus in love and are not serving Him. They are a target for the evil one.

Oftentimes people guard their comfort zone at all costs. They don't want to get involved. Let someone else do it. The problem is that there are not enough people concerned about actual ministry. It is easier not to get involved. It is going to cost you energy and the bearing of others' burdens to get involved. Sadly, many Christians never step into ministry and bear little fruit. They will be held accountable one day (2 Corinthians 5:10) and may not receive any rewards or commendation in heaven. (1 Corinthians 3:14-15; Matthew 25:23) The scripture in Galatians 6 goes on in the following verse to say, "Bear one another's burdens and so fulfill the law of Christ." Many churches will do anything to avoid conflict. However, it does take much wisdom and grace to deal with these difficult and sometimes divisive issues, because pride can still be alive among Christians. Much teaching is needed. Some churches are too safe to live and preach the gospel.

The second approach is to truly believe that there can be full restoration and are champions of the people that need to be supported and restored. "Above all, keep loving one another earnestly, since love covers a multitude of sins" (1 Peter 4:8) This kind of love release us from the root sins of pride and envy, etc. in our own lives. "And after you have suffered a little while, the God of all grace, who has called you to his eternal glory in Christ, will restore, confirm, strengthen, and establish you" (1 Peter 5:10) "Let love be genuine. Abhor what is evil; hold fast to what is good" (Romans 12:9). These are God's ways and His instructions to us.

"Let him know that whoever brings back a sinner from his wandering will save his soul from death and will cover a multitude of sins" (James 5:20) He will save his soul from death because it is truly truth lived out, it is a confirmation of our election in Christ and it releases us from sin. The love of God always releases us from sin. For if they fall, one will lift up his fellow. But woe to him who is alone when he falls and has not another to lift him up!" (Ecclesiastes 4:10)

Jesus said, "By this, all people will know that you are my disciples if you have a love for one another" (John 13:35) How we treat people, especially our Christian brother and sister, backs up our proclamation of the gospel. If we just toss people aside how is that love? Jesus also said, "If you love those who love you, what reward is that to you? Do not even the tax collectors do the same?

And if you greet only your brothers, what more are you doing than others? Do not even the Gentiles do the same? You, therefore, must be perfect, as your heavenly Father is perfect" (Matthew 5:46-48). We cannot have a truly close fellowship in churches if we don't truly care for one another. This is one of Christ's greatest witnesses to the world. A close fellowship in grace and truth in a church certainly brings glory to Christ.

How we treat other people is noticed. How we treat one another has a great impact. People especially observe how we treat others in need because we all are in need sometimes and people reason that if they treated these other people with grace, they will also likely treat me likewise. This results in a close fellowship. In a world that is primarily transactional—what you can do for me—this is noticed. If we can't even treat our Christian brother with grace, how can we be trusted with the hearts of others in crisis? As someone has said in a song, "If we don't even love our friends, how will we love our enemies."

Wayne Grudem in his excellent book called, *What the Bible Says About Divorce and Remarriage*, states some of the reasons or exceptions that might make a divorce a legitimate possibility. Grudem's book is the most thorough book of the many books I have read on the

Biblical and theological issue of divorce and remarriage. He used to have a more legalistic view but came to realize that the scriptures were not truly teaching this approach.

The foundation scripture that Grudem uses to come to his Biblical and theological understanding is 1 Corinthians 7:10-16 as the Apostle Paul states:

"To the married, I give this charge (not I, but the Lord): the wife should not separate from her husband (but if she does, she should remain unmarried or else be reconciled to her husband), and the husband should not divorce his wife. To the rest, I say (I, not the Lord) that if any brother has a wife who is an unbeliever, and she consents to live with him, he should not divorce her. If any woman has a husband who is an unbeliever, and he consents to live with her, she should not divorce him. For the unbelieving husband is made holy because of his wife, and the unbelieving wife is made holy because of her husband. Otherwise, your children would be unclean, but as it is, they are holy. But if the unbelieving partner separates, let it be so. In such cases, *the brother or sister is not enslaved. God has called you to peace. For how do you know, wife, whether you will save your husband? Or how do you know, husband, whether you will save your wife?"*

In this case, the Apostle Paul makes an exception for the case of desertion. If the non-Christian spouse deserts the other spouse, they are free to live in peace, and although often, not always, this would mean remarriage. If the Apostle makes room for an exception because of this there could be other cases since people still harden their hearts today and maliciously do evil one to another. Those who are called Christians and those who are not. Grudem stresses the term Paul uses in verse 15 "in such cases." If there are these cases it implies that there could be other causes. This could include of course adultery even though there can be forgiveness and restoration when there is actually repentance. It could also include divorce for abuse, physical and emotional, theft, etc., etc. "No book on Christian ethics can possibly specify all the complex details that will be part of every real-life situation."[1] Imagine trying to explain in a couple of sentences the complexity of a person's unique situation and have people make a judgment on it. This would be very inconsiderate and uncompassionate.

"Extreme, prolonged verbal and relational cruelty: Treatment that is destroying the other spouse's mental and emotional stability could be so severe that it would

---

1 Ibid, 35

fall into the category of "in such cases" and would be a legitimate ground for divorce."[2] Men have a hard time admitting and sharing about the emotional abuse of their wives and their oftentimes malicious manipulation because men have to be men and should know how to graciously lead. They don't want to admit what may be their failure or perceived as their failure to lead. They most likely don't want to talk about it with others that they don't absolutely trust or feel they have some great skill in counseling and grace, especially if they do harm. Fortunately, we can always dialogue with the Lord and He can be our counselor. (John 14:26)

"In some way, such abuse is worse than desertion because it involves repeated demonstration of actual malice, not simply indifference. Abuse is actively malevolent. And the result is the same (the couple is no longer together) the abusing spouse has not deserted but he or she bears the moral built of causing the separation." [3] Emotional abandonment in a marriage is a very risky place for a relationship to be in a state. There can be many temptations and broken fences brought into the

---

2 Ibid, 34

3 Grudem, 37

relationship that may be very difficult to repair later on. Again, the Apostle Paul says in God's word to a married couple, "The husband should give to his wife her conjugal rights, and likewise the wife to her husband. For the wife does not have authority over her own body, but the husband does. Likewise, the husband does not have authority over his own body, but the wife does. Do not deprive one another, except perhaps by agreement for a limited time, that you may devote yourself to prayer; but then come together again, so that Satan may not tempt you because of your lack of self-control" (1 Corinthians 7:3-5). Couples are not to use sex as a means of manipulation in a marriage.

Grudem proposes rightly that, "God allowed divorce as a remedy in some cases where marriages were irreparably damaged."[4] "Divorce because the Marriage can't be repaired? Should a divorce be granted when a husband and wife have been strongly alienated from each other for many months or years and their entrenched hostility against each other has not responded to repeated attempts at counseling and reconciliation? In such a situation, people who know the couple might say that the marriage is beyond repair. Craig Blomberg

---

4 Ibid, 16

apparently advocated this position for severely damaged marriages, He wrote: "Perhaps the best way of describing when divorce and remarriage are permitted, then is to say simply that it is when an individual, in agreement with a supportive Christian community of which that individual has been an intimate part, believes that he or she has no other choice or option in trying to avoid some greater evil. All known attempts at reconciliation have been exhausted." [5]

The ideal for a couple is married for a lifetime. This takes a lot of forgiveness and restoration, it takes a love fueled by the ideal and compassion, consideration, and seeking the best for the other and the relationship. However, the ideal doesn't always happen. People sin. You and I sin, even though we have been justified by faith alone in Christ Jesus. We should always be growing but no one is without sin before and after salvation. As R.C. Ryle stated: "Many appear to forget that we are saved and justified sinners, and only as sinners; and that we can never attain to anything higher if we live to the age

---

5 Craig Blomber, "Marriage, Divorce, Remarriage and Celibacy: An Exegsis of Matthew 19:3-12, "TrinJ, n.s. 11 (1990): 193. Cited in Grudem p. 43

of Methuselah. Redeemed sinners, justified sinners, and renewed sinners doubtless we must be, --but sinners, sinners, always to the very last." They do not seem to comprehend that there is a wide difference between our justification and our sanctification. Our justification is a perfect finished work and admits not degrees. Our sanctification is imperfect and incomplete, and will be till the last hour of our life." [6] However, the Bible also calls us saints. Saints are the ones who are in Christ. They have righteousness in Christ, not in themselves. However, a true Christian will be making some progress in sanctification. (Matthew 12:20) Even the well know and fruitful evangelist in the 17th Century John Wesley was divorced.

Even though we shoot for the ideal we live in a fallen world and evil can still at times affect us. However, as we confess and continue on in the Lord, he progressively cleanses us. (1 John 1:9) We have to be realistic as well in our approach to life. The ideal doesn't always entirely depend and us or us in the Lord. In this light, Thomas Cranmer in the 15th Century who eventually was burned

---

6 R.C. Ryle, Assurance, (Evangelical Press, 1989), pp. 94-95. Cited in John Benton, Evangelistic Calvinism, (Carlisle, PA: Banner of Truth, 2006) 32

at the stake for his stand with Protestantism and as a former archbishop of Canterbury states the legitimate and non-legitimate reasons for divorce and remarriage in his book, *Reformatio Legum Ecclesiasticarum* (1553). He ministered during the time of Henry the VIII. Here are the five legitimate reasons for divorce and remarriage:

1. Adultery
2. Desertion with malice.
3. Prolonged absence without news.
4. Deadly hostility
5. Ill-treatment

Even the Puritans who are primarily known for the precision in Theology, experience, and its application had a more realistic approach. The Puritan era it seems to me was a Providential time of great blessings that lasted almost 100 years, but towards the end may have moved in some to a more legalistic approach. It was not the case, especially for the Puritan William Ames.

Grudem states: "There is a very well-known Puritan writer named William Ames, who was a highly respected ethics instructor, and he's writing around the time the King James version was first published. And he said, "If one party drive away, the other with great fierceness and cruelty, there is the cause of desertion and he has reputed the deserter. But if obstinately neglect, that necessary departure of the other who is avoiding the imminent danger, he himself, in that situation, is the deserter." So, William Ames is saying if someone is physically or emotionally abusing his or her spouse so that the other person has to flee for self-protection, it's the abuser who is guilty of the desertion or the separation, not the person who has left. A marriage may be dissolved in those cases."

Grudem in the same article also states: "I went back even earlier than the early Puritan period to a church father named Chrysostom, writing in the late 300 AD and early 400s. He says this about marriage in his commentary on 1 Corinthians, "If day by day he punched you, and keep up worse or fighting on this account, it is better to separate" and then he quotes Paul, "that God has called us to peace for it is the other party who furnished the ground of separation, even as he did who committed uncleanness." So, he seems to be saying at least separation and perhaps divorce.

The great truth is wrapped up in the Biblical teaching of the "Priesthood of the believers." The Bible says in this regard: "But you are a chosen race, a royal priesthood, a holy nation, a people for his own possession, that you may proclaim the excellencies of him who called you out of darkness into his marvelous light" (1 Peter 2:9). He is addressing Christians in the verse. We as his people don't need to go through a priest to commune with God or find direction in life we can go directly to the word of God and also be directed by the Holy Spirit and at times wise Godly counselors or spiritual directors. This freedom to go directly to Jesus is a wonderful privilege. However, it is healthy to confess our sins to one another as is appropriate as the scripture states in James 5:16. This should be a person that is gracious, wise, Theological, and can keep confidences. One you can trust with your heart and confidences.

The problem comes in when we think we are experts on everything but perhaps not have taken up the hard task of studying theology. Theology is the process of putting all the parts of divine revelation together as a whole for understanding. Therefore, we don't correctly interpret God's word or we also don't discern the Spirits leading. Everyone does what is right in their own eyes, not based on good Theology or right doctrine, but often on the world's opinions, the desires of the flesh, or other uninformed Christians. However, the study of theology is not made easy by having various Godly people coming to varying conclusions. However, we are not just to shut down our thinking, reasoning, and discerning ability just because it is hard. One day each of us will give an account of how we have handled God's word and the Holy Spirit. As God's word says: "Do your best to present yourself to God as one approved, a worker, who has no need to be ashamed, rightly handling the word of truth" (2 Timothy 2:15). Teachers of God's word will have even greater accountability. "Not many of you should become teachers, my brothers, for you know that we who teach will be judged with a greater strictness" (James 3:1)

Let me say to round out this section that we should always hold out the ideal for marriage and strive toward it. Divorce causes much harm to many people but sometimes in wisdom, it cannot be avoided. "No matter what circumstances led up to this present marriage, if you are married, you are now married to the right person, and God wants you to make that marriage a good one for the rest of your life." [7]

Threatening divorce or separation should never be used as a tact of manipulation or just because of careless words. This causes a negative element to the relationship

---

7 Grudem, 60

that should be avoided. It opens the door to exploring options that may not be helpful, and Satan is quick to jump on this bandwagon and encourage this direction.

CHAPTER SEVEN

Leadership When Divorced and Remarried

Now we get to where what we really believe shows up. It is where the rubber meets the road. Pastoral ministry can be really hard on a marriage. People expect that they can act very non-Christian but the pastor and his wife are to be very Christian. It is often a one-way relationship. This can be quite draining. The pastor is an imperfect human being just like everyone else, even though he is called by God to be in public ministry. Every Christian is called to ministry but some are called to leadership in ministry. However, because God calls people to the ministry, these people with the love of God in their hearts, love to serve God and His people. However, pastoral ministry can be especially difficult for the wife. Much harm can be done to a pastor's family because of mistreatment by the congregation or the lack of skill in the leadership of the Pastor. Hopefully, with the help of others, the Pastor can learn about leadership and the church can learn about ministry and leadership, as well. It is hard for a wife to see her husband and family mistreated.

Those involved in ministry are standard bearers standing out in front and are prime targets for the enemy the devil. Everyone in ministry or actually practicing following Jesus is a target. Better to be a target than to be lulled in a dangerous and guilty silence and inaction and to be denied the fulness in Christ. A pastor is encouraged by a church that holds him up and his family in prayer as the men in the time of Moses held up Moses' hands in prayer. (Exodus 17:12) We must be people of a life of prayer if we are to stand against the evil one and advance in the face of opposition and push back the gates of hell. This is where spiritual formation is desperately important and essential. "God opposes the proud but gives grace to the humble. Submit yourselves therefore to God. Resist the devil, and he will flee from you. Draw near to God, and he will draw near to you" (James 4:6-7). We should be careful not to make the ministry a burden to those in ministry and not to discourage but encourage them and their families and add to their lives as they add to ours. We should all pray every day for humility and for laborers for the harvest as Jesus instructed us. (Matthew 9:35-38)

We are in a special covenant relationship in marriage and especially with God. It is not healthy if it is only one way. We are in a Covenant relationship with each other as Christians and especially in the local church to which we belong. A covenant is a two-way relationship and love agreement.

Are those who have been divorced and remarried disqualified for ministry? There are some who definitely think so. There is another school of thought who believes that a pastor can and should be fully restored to pastoral ministry. If the marriage broke down and the pastor is remarried and is now a Godly person largely in his heart and actions he can be restored to ministry.

Some people believe that a pastor who has been divorced and or remarried is not above reproach. Does this mean that the persons making the judgment are above reproach? Are they without sin? Do they not sin in word, action, motive, and thought every day? We are not like the world which seek to punish people and judge people for the rest of their life because of some failure. We truly believe in the power of God working within a true believer and letting God bring good out of a bad situation. (Romans 8:28) The point is that the person considered for a leadership role in the church should be living a Godly life now and have a true and purifying love for God and others. They should, however, be above blatant reproach for how they are now. None are above reproach if that means being perfect.

Some would point to the Old Testament and say that in the Old Testament a priest could not be divorced. (Leviticus 21:7) Yes, they were not to marry a prostitute or a divorced woman, but they could only marry a virgin. (Leviticus 21:14) Is this what is practiced today—I think not. We, however, are no longer under the ceremonial law but the moral law as it is fully revealed in this age of grace for Christians in, Jesus Christ. There are no longer priests in Evangelical Christianity, there are pastors, teachers, and evangelists. (Ephesians 4:11) There are imperfect people called to a very holy calling as are all Christians, but they are called to lead.

The qualifications listed in Christian leadership are listed in 1 Timothy 3:1-13: Titus 1:5-9. In these scriptures along with other guidelines, there is the stated that they should be "the husband of one wife." What does this mean? Is he talking about a person who has been divorced and remarried? I don't believe this is the right interpretation. If this was the case he would have said so, and I don't believe God is wrapping all the possible situations into one statement. How about those who are not married, are they disqualified for leadership? I believe however this statement does envelope the issue of polygamy, which was very important but the phrase one wife literally means in Greek, "a one-woman husband." He is not a man who is flirting with other women. His eye is focused on his wife. He is a man loyal to his wife according to God's set priorities. If he is divorced and remarried, he should only be loyal and devoted to one woman at a time—a one-woman man.

Also, according to these scriptures, they are general guidelines. How about a Christian leader whose children after they have grown up are not following the Lord? Each person has free will and can go God's way or the devil's way. We cannot control a person's will although, we can have a great influence on them. Let us be reasonable in considering a pastor and his family and not expect them to be what we ourselves are not willing to be, and if we are Christlike, we will seek to build them up rather than tear them down.

When a person's children are younger it is reasonable to expect that they attend church and follow the parent's guidelines, not being neglected for lack of instruction and direction.

Conclusion

It seems that there are three overall approaches to this whole revelation of God's word the Bible and to living the Christian life. The first approach is a focus on the law and this is legalism. The second approach is to focus on grace without the law and this is antinomianism or liberalism, the third approach is to focus on law and gospel and this is the true gospel, couched in grace. My approach is the focus on law and gospel and to hold them in balance according to the whole Biblical revelation and rightly apply them. As the scripture says we are to rightly divide them. (2 Timothy 2:15) This means we are to rightly divide law and gospel and their application and use. Of course, the primary focus is on grace.

Too many come to saving faith by grace and then go back to having their primary focus of living by the law and in their own strength rather than in Christ's strength. In this approach, there is the standard of grace for ourselves and law for others. The law tells us what sin is and our need for God and the gospel offers us grace to be spiritually raised from the dead and to walk in the newness of life in Christ. We need to find the balance and we can find it in the Biblical revelation and in the Holy Spirit.

The approach we take will affect our relationship with God and others. It will do harm or it will restore people to the fulness of life that God wants for them. We will either encourage people in the Lord or discourage them by our legalism and antinomianism. Our approach will either be the law or grace or law and gospel rightly divided and applied. We are either going to be like Christ, sinners, or the Pharisees. If our approach is like the Pharisees, it will be an overemphasis on the law without the gospel.

Jesus in the parable of the talents states that the master is displeased with the servant who because he was afraid of the risk buried his talent in the ground. That is the state of most churches today. They don't want to take any risks in ministry—it might divide people and cause conflict. They are not vulnerable enough to truly love. We must take risks to love. We must take risks in the restoration business. God is not honored when we consider one of his people not worth the bother. It is easier to go with those who don't seem to have as many problems. Even the evangelical church today is losing attendees because we are not displaying God's gospel in the church. If we want only to reach those with few problems how is that the gospel? We are not going to reach the world with a legalistic approach.

Those who are in business know about moving ahead in spite of experiencing at times many failures. Those who succeed often fail, especially in business or inventions before they are successful. They take risks. Hopefully, wise and calculated risks, but often fearless risks to accomplish great things. How are we to bring the gospel to the world if we do not extend it by our life to one another? We are to take care of our wounded soldiers not just abandon them.

Christianity is a counter-culture and transforms culture. Today we have gone along with the culture to a fault, thinking that by being like them we will win them to Christ and his gospel. However, God wants us to like Him and He will draw people to himself. Like the world, people easily go down the road of fault-finding so that they can excuse themselves and feel better about themselves or think they are better than others. (Luke 18:9-12)

Divorce and remarriage and leadership were legal in the Old Testament. Jesus expands his grace in relation to the law, are we then making a new law harsher law than the Old Testament?

Martin Luther's insistence on understanding the distinction between the law and gospel he believed was the most important distinction in understanding the whole of the Bible. In preaching evangelistic and gospel messages we must have both the law and the gospel to rightly preach God's gospel as William Perkins clearly explains in his book, *The Art of Prophesying*. If we are not preaching and teaching the law and gospel and the right division and use of them, we are not declaring the gospel. We must understand the bad news to even comprehend the good news. Martin Luther basically said that if one can understand the proper distinction between the law and gospel and its application that person should be given a Ph.D. in Theology. To the people that make everything about liberty he said, "Thus dear friends, I have said it clearly enough, and I believe you ought to understand it and not make liberty a law." However, we are under the Royal law of Christ? "Bear one another burdens, and so fulfill the law of Christ" (Galatians 6:2)

Jesus said to the Pharisees, "You blind guides, straining out a gnat and swallowing a camel" (Matthew 23:26). The Pharisees were very, very concerned about keeping the law. They developed laws upon laws to ensure that they and others kept the law, but they missed the main point. The law was not an end in itself it was pointing to a greater reality which is God Himself. God wants the best for us and offers us grace and a new heart to walk in the fulness of God's purposes. Our general orientation can be towards the Royal law of Christ or the law often added to by man, like the Pharisees. However, God's law and gospel must be held together and the distinctions must be understood and applied., Yes, we need both but they must be held in balance and applied with great discernment. (Romans 10:4) Otherwise, we also will miss out on God's best for us and others and will not bring Him glory. It is especially important to remember that we are in a day of God's expanded grace in the fulness of His revelation in Jesus Christ.

Many get saved by grace but then go back to having their overall orientation to the law rather than grace. No wonder they tend to be judgemental. As Martin Luther implied this issue of law and gospel will not be taught in an hour-long presentation, but it will take deep and graceful study. We don't want to become the new Pharisees. This understanding of the distinction between law and gospel and the application thereof and critical to healthy Christianity. This teaching is largely missing in today's evangelical church. Theology makes a difference in our relationship with God and the quality of our life both Systematic and Spiritual Theology, which takes time and great diligence. As J.I. Packer stated in a similar context it is not like getting an order of fries in a brown paper bag to go.

We need to seriously take a look at this controversial issue related to the Biblical Theology of the whole Bible and make sure we understand it in context. We must understand the different contexts of the literary devices to communicate the move beautiful truth of God and His grace in mercy amidst His holiness and justice. We are not to be the judge God is. We do not see their hearts as God does. We consider people's lives now not based on our judgments of their past entirely or think we have to judge if they are worthy. If their lives are not perfect enough now you may pass on them, although, God may have more grace than his people. He restores people. He truly loves people and knows by His power great things can be brought to be, and humble people can glorify Him. He also resists the proud. (James 4:6)

Let us display Christ by our heart, our actions, including our words and our Theology, and His love. Those without Christ can be restored to life in Christ and those in Christ can be restored to fullness in Christ.

The world will know we are Christians by the quality and the theological and experiential depth of our love. "By this, all people will know that you are my disciples if you love one another" (John 13:35) Let the church truly be the church and follow Christ fully and thus bring glory to His full beauty, power, justice, and love. The world is watching how we treat one another. Does the world believe us if we can't truly love those in the church? Can they really believe that we will like the world only posture love? God is calling His people and the church to fulness in Him. (Ephesians 4:1) Let us rightly divide God's word between the law and gospel and rightly apply it, in the foundation of His grace. It seems to me that this issue of divorce and remarriage exposes and is one of the dividing lines between legalism or the law and gospel rightly applied.

APPENDIX
BIBLIOGRAPHY

Armstrong John H., *Can Fallen Pastors Be Restored? The Church Response to Sexual Misconduct*, (Chicago: Moody Press, 1995)

Adams Jay E., *Marriage, Divorce, and Remarriage in the Bible*, (Grand Rapids, MI: Zondervan Publishers, 1980)

Beek Joel, R, Smally Paul M., *Reformed Systematic Theology*, (Wheaton, Illinois: Crossway) 2019

Brauns Chris, *Unpacking Forgiveness: Biblical Answers for Complex Questions and Deep Wounds*, (Wheaton, Illinois: Crossway Books, 2208)

House, Wayne H., editor, *Divorce, and Remarriage: Four Christian Views*, (Downers Grove, IL: Intervarsity Press, 1990)

Instone-Brewer, David, *Divorce, and Remarriage in the Bible: The Social and Literary Context*, (Grand Rapids, Michigan: Eerdmans, 2002)

Instone-Brewer, David, *Divorce, and Remarriage in the Church: Biblical Solutions for Pastoral Realities*, (Carlisle, Cumbria, Uk: Paternoster Press, 2003)

Keener Craig S., *And Marries Another: Divorce and Remarriage in the Teaching of the New Testament*, (Peabody, Massachusetts: Hendrickson Publishers, 1991

LaHaye Tim, *If Ministers Fall, Can They be Restored?* (Grand Rapids, Michigan: Pyranee Books, 1990)

Maxwell John C., *Failing Forward: Turning Mistakes Into Stepping Stones for Success*, (Nashville, Tennessee: Nelson Books, 2000)

Niebergal Alan J., *Enjoying God: Prayer and Spiritual Formation,* (BooXAi, 2022)

Niebergal, Alan, J., *Right With God: The Basics,* (Bloomington IN: Authorhouse, 2012)

Perkins William, *The Art of Prophesying*, (Carlisle, Pennsylvania: Banner of Trust, 1996)

Piper John, Grudem Wayne, *Recovering Biblical Manhood & Womanhood*, (Wheaton IL: Crossway, 2012)

Richards, Larry, *Remarriage: A Healing Gift from God*, (Waco, Texas: Word Books, 1981)

Ramm Bernard, *Protestant Biblical Interpretation*, (Grand Rapids, MI: Baker Academic, 1950)

Small, Dwight Hervey, *Remarriage and God's Renewing Grace: A Positive Biblical Ethic for Divorced People*, (Grand Rapids, Michigan: Baker Book House, 1986)

ALSO BY

ALAN J. NIEBERGAL

Right with God: The Basics

ISBN 978-1477274040

Published in 2012 with AuthorHouse

This book is about being right with God now and to eternity. It is based on a relationship with God through Jesus Christ that brings us into a fulfilling relationship with Him. This book talks about the basic truths that can assist everyone to be right with God and grow in that relationship in Christ.

Enjoying God: Prayer and Spiritual Formation

ASIN : B0B752WTJN

Published in 2022, with BooxAi

This book is about experiencing the greatest blessings of this life and the life to come. It is about the beautiful spiritual blessings of Jesus in heavenly places. It is the road to fullness and wholeness. It is the road that anyone who has a healthy self-interest will choose. This life of fullness is entered into by developing in the Lord, a life of prayer.

CPSIA information can be obtained
at www.ICGtesting.com
Printed in the USA
BVHW090833140922
646857BV00001B/56

9 781990 389191